Creative Prob
Techniques ....ge
Your Life

©Colin G Smith 2013
http://www.AwesomeMindSecrets.com

Disclaimer:

This eBook is for educational purposes only, and is not intended to
be a substitute for professional counselling, therapy or medical
treatment. Nothing in this eBook is intended to diagnose or treat any
pathology or diseased condition of the mind or body. The author will
not be held responsible for any results of reading or applying the
information.

Table of Contents

About Colin G Smith

For over ten years now I have been driven to find the very best methods for creating effective personal change. If you are anything like me, you're probably interested in simple and straight-forward explanations. Practical stuff that gets results! I am a NLP Master Practitioner, writer & author who has written several books including:

- *Boost Your Mind Power: 99+ Awesome Mind Power Techniques*

- *How To Relieve Stress In Your Daily Life Using The Emotional Freedom Technique (EFT)*

- *Neuro-Linguistic Programming NLP Techniques - Quick Start Guide*

Visit My Amazon Author Page:

Amazon.com/Colin-G-Smith/e/B00A3HEKOM

What Is Creative Thinking and Creative Problem Solving?

You know the human mind, your mind, is truly awesome. Everything we see around us, incredible architecture, paintings, wondrous machines and the amazing musical masterpieces of the ages all started in someone's imagination!

So what is creative thinking?

It's the ability to re-arrange, re-formulate, re-pattern, mix, merge and construct already known and new 'thought forms' in different combinations.

We all possess this creative mechanism.

Sometimes though we become, *"stuck in a rut"* or start to, *"see blank"*, or we *"hit a brick wall."* These are common phrases used by people that are in 'stuck states.' Their mind is unwilling to go elsewhere.

Creativity is just a state of mind that can be triggered with specific mental strategies and can be enhanced by exploring other perspectives using a variety of tools. And the great thing is, the more you practice creative thinking techniques, the more creative you become!

By learning to use our brains in more diverse ways we can discover the keys to unlocking the power of our creative imagination!

As you read on you will discover many wonderful ways to use your mind to solve problems creatively...

Creative Thinking Exercises That Will Pull You Out of a Creativity Quagmire Quickly!

It has been said that all we are ever really doing is pulling things apart or putting things back together. You could say, 'there are no new ideas under the sun.' However there are an infinite number of ways we can combine ideas together into interesting new combinations or 'recipes.'

When you are 'stuck in a rut' or creatively blocked your mind is locked into just one limited perspective. Discovering new angles on the project you are working on enables you to gain creative insight.

We all have internal mental strategies such as Decision, Motivation and of course Creative strategies. This usually functions outside of our awareness, but we can identify the step by step unconscious process and then trigger it when ever we want!

One day I was sat in a coffee shop, with pen & pad and laptop, hoping to write an article. I struggled for a while and nothing was really transpiring. So I thought, *"Hmmmm, what is it like when I feel really inspired?"*

I then remembered a time I was crossing a desert, right out in the middle of nowhere. There was nothing apart from a road, sand and a few shrubs for hundreds of miles. In the evening I stopped the Jeep, turned the lights off and stepped out…

Have you ever been to a Planetarium? Well this was like the best Planetarium in the world! There was no light pollution whatsoever. You could see stars right to the very horizon in every direction. The more you looked up at the stars, the more appeared. The Milky Way was crystal clear. It was truly wondrous! It felt like being connected into the vast, vast Universe.

So what I did next was I took inventory of how I created that state of awe and wonder in my mind. I noticed the image in my mind was true to life size, 360 degrees around me and clear. I also noticed my internal dialogue saying, *"Wow, this is amazing!"* and then noticed the feelings in my body.

What I did next was think about my writing project; Noticed the visual, auditory and kinaesthetic aspects to it and then mapped then across into the 'Wow' experience. I actually saw sheets of paper 360 degrees around me and in the milky way with writing appearing on them while my self talk was saying, *"Wow, that's amazing!"*

As soon as I did this shift in perspective my feelings shifted into feeling good and inspired. Literally within moments of doing that creative thinking exercise I was able to write in a way that was flowing and inspired.

So what I did was become aware of one of my 'creative thinking recipes.' Why not do some creative thinking activities and discover one of your recipes or give mine a go and see what results you get? Here is my strategy in step-by-step format:

Technique: Escaping A Creativity Quagmire Quickly!

1. Ask yourself, "*Hmmmm, what is it like when I feel really inspired?*"

2. I recalled a time when I was out in the desert with nothing around for hundreds of miles apart from the road, sand and a few shrubs. In the evening I parked up, turned the lights off and just stood watching the amazing night sky.

3. The next thing I did was take inventory of the way I represented that memory in my mind - My Internal Representations:

I saw through my own eyes. The image was life size, crisp clarity and fully surrounding me 360 degrees.

I had an internal voice that said, "*Wow, this is amazing!*"

And then I noticed the feelings in my body:

Quite a fast spinning, rolling forward sensation from my hands to my stomach to my heart, looping back around again and again. I'd call it excitement.

4. What I did next was to think about my creative block. I saw a blank sheet of paper and my internal dialogue was like, "*urrrrgggghhh.*"

5. I then 'Mapped Across' that representation into the "Wow" experience: I actually saw sheets of paper 360 degrees around me and in the milky way with writing appearing on them while my self talk was saying, "*Wow, that's amazing!*"

As soon as I did this shift in perspective my feelings shifted into feeling good and inspired. Literally within moments of doing this creative thinking exercise I was able to write in a way that was flowing and inspired!

The Structure Of Thought

Your mind is working all the time, even while you sleep. Of the many and varied thought process's that flow through your mind-stream every day, they can only be made up of the same basic building blocks; Images, sounds, feelings, smells and tastes. All of your memories, thought habit patterns and conceptions about the future are made of these 5 elements.

One of the most important discoveries in recent years into how our consciousness functions and how we can use that knowledge for practical purposes came from the field of Neuro-Linguistic Programming (NLP). It had been observed before but it wasn't until Dr. Bandler and Dr. Grinder came along that the systematic analysis of how we code our internal representations was observed and made explicit. This became known as the Model of Sub-Modalities.

All of this is easier than it sounds. Take for example the pleasant memory of a holiday experience. If you were to think about that now, you may begin to remember being on the beach on a hot summer day, blue sky, seagulls and the sound of the lapping waves. Now if you were to pay closer attention to the imagery you were making in your minds eye (*internal representations*), you could notice how big the image is, how close the image is, whether it is still or moving and so on. There are a number of these visual qualities you can observe. Here is a partial list:

- Colour or B/W
- Near or Far
- Bright or Dim
- Location
- Size of Picture
- Associated or Disassociated
- Focused
- Framed or Panoramic
- Moving or Still
- Movie Speed

- 3D or 2D
- Viewing Angle
- No. of Pictures

Now what's really important about becoming aware of this 'sub-modality coding' is that you are in fact becoming aware of your deep sub-conscious process's. And you can use this knowledge to do some really cool things! Like making boring, mundane tasks fun!

Think about this: How do you know the difference between a good memory and a bad memory? Your mind somehow has to code these memories differently. It does this by using different sub-modalities. One of the quickest ways to become aware of these coding's is to compare two memories together; a contrastive analysis.

To give an example, I'll use a bad memory experience of waiting at an uncovered train platform in the rain with a considerable delay. The good memory is being on holiday on a warm beach. Now by paying attention to the two images we can notice the difference in their qualities or sub-modalities.

As you can see below I've just listed four sub-modalities to make it easier:

Bad Memory
- Location: To the left
- Associated / Disassociated: Disassociated (I can see myself in the image.)
- Colour/Black & White: Dim Colours
- Distance / Size: Small and further away

Good Memory

- Location: To the right
- Associated / Disassociated: Associated (I am seeing through my eyes.)
- Colour/Black & White: Bright colours
- Distance / Size: Bigger and closer

These 'codings' are the difference that makes the difference. It's these characteristics that create the feelings you have. So when you know how, you can change them to change your habitual responses.

For example a 'bad memory' of a dismal rainy day stuck at the train station could be a small, disassociated, distant, black and white image, while one of your pleasant holiday experience memories is big, bright, associated, colourful and moving.

Now we can use this knowledge to 're-program' our experiences. If you were to take that bad memory and move it into the same location as the good memory and transform it's qualities into 'associated,' 'brighter colours,' and 'bigger and closer,' you would find yourself feeling much better about that bad memory even though the context of the representation remains the same. It's the sub-modalities that count!

There is a lot you can do with just the information you've learned above. How useful would it be to be able to transform your memories of future mundane work tasks into enthusiasm and gusto? This is quite easy to do…

Technique: Mundanity Into Enthusiasm

1. Think about a specific memory of a mundane task you have to do.

2. Think about an activity that fills you with enthusiasm and curiosity.

3. Now do a contrastive analysis: Notice the differences between the two images. Are they in different locations in space? Is one closer than the other? Is one a moving image and the other still? (*Draw a vertical line on paper and jot down the differences between the two images.*)

4. When you've discovered the coding differences look at your 'mundane memory' and shift it over into the location of 'enthusiasm.' Change it's sub-modalities so that they are the coding's

11

of enthusiasm; Bigger, brighter, closer, moving images…

That's it. But because the mind gets into habits it's best to do this on a few more memories to help train or program the mind into the new coding's. You can do this easily enough by thinking about three or more similar future mundane tasks that are coming up and map them across into the coding's of enthusiasm. Doing so makes good use of the 'generalisation effect' of the mind.

You can use this method to transform any memory into something more resourceful. Here's more ideas for you:

- Humiliation into Laughter (*"One day you will be able to laugh at this."*)
- Unsociable into Friendliness
- Boredom into Curiosity
- Defeated into Self Determination
- Frustration into Inspiration
- Indifference into Loving
- Doubt into Possibility (For your new goals?!)

What others can you come up with?

How to Access The Wisdom of Your Future Self

What would be the best advice that you could receive from your wiser future self?

A great imagination experiment to do is to pretend to step into a you from the future, it could be a couple of decades from now or, if you allow yourself to be open enough, future lives!

Doing so can reveal amazing insights that will profit you in the here and now.

One of the amazing things about reality is that Time doesn't really exist. There is only the present moment. If we think about a past event, we are of course, really experiencing a representation of that event in 'the now.'

By using our mind we can create an approximation of the future. And it could be LIFETIMES from now! Such is the power of our imagination.

Let's say you are doing a project and could use some creative insight. By stepping into a 'future self' you can look back at that person in the 'present' and ask questions to gain insight in how to move forward.

As the future self ask:

- *"What does that person need to do to solve that problem quickly and easily?"*
- *"What kind of person does he need to become to resolve that issue?"*
- *"What does that person need to do to move forward?"*
- *"What would that you have to have learned in order to solve that problem?"*

Let's face it – problems are going to keep coming. So we need to

13

maintain a powerful determination.

What would happen if you were to imagine having a conversation with your wiser future self, gaining a new understanding of how to keep motivated and determined?

If you were to step into that wiser self you could also experience those feelings of determination and resolve.

What happens if you were to do that now and then allow an image to appear that represents those feelings.

Now you can pass that gift (the image) to your present self. Where in your body would it be best to store that resource? Your heart?

You can then tap into those positive feelings any time you feel the need by bringing the image to mind and allowing those feelings to arise.

Can you think of any specific situations in the future where it would be useful to experience those resourceful feelings?

Pick one: And then notice what the first thing you would see is. Maybe it's a door or a logo sign.

As you hold that thought, bring to mind the symbol you came up with for the resource and feel those good feelings as they become associated with the first thing you will see in that upcoming situation.

Why not do this for 3 other situations so the process generalises…

Making Mistakes In Life – How To Move On

Making mistakes in life is inevitable. It's how you react to 'failure' that makes the difference. Your brain/mind is an incredible learning machine that knows how to learn from mistakes. Making a mistake doesn't have to mean failure. They can be great opportunities to learn something of value. You probably know already that one of the character traits of great achievers is that of...

Technique: *"There is no Failure Only Feedback"*

1. Think of something in your life where you think you have failed.

2. Now as you think about it, ask yourself, *"What can I learn from that experience that is useful?" "What do I know now that I did not know before?" "And what else?"*

*There is always something new and useful to learn.

Simple Self Hypnosis Secrets That Can Change Your Life Today!

Psychologists and Doctors used to send their 'impossible' clients to him and in many instances he helped them to turn their lives around. Dr. Milton H. Erickson was one of the most successful hypnotherapists in the world and is often referred to as *'the father of modern hypnosis.'*

One of the factors that set him apart from other change workers was his strong faith in the potential of human beings. He knew that when a person stopped stumbling around with their conscious mind and tapped into the limitless ocean of unconscious resources, people could make wonderful changes.

He used to look at a client and say, *"You've tried to solve this problem with your conscious mind and failed utterly. Now is the time to access your unconscious resources in a way that resolves this problem effectively."*

One of the common misconceptions about self hypnosis is that you have to be able to concentrate and go into a profoundly altered state. This could be done, however what we are really interested in is accessing other areas of our mind (i.e. unconscious resources) so that we can make certain changes giving rise to our chosen outcome.

The good news is you can do this very easily and you can give it a go now with the following techniques. No need for deep trance!

Technique: Three Magic Doors

This is a classic hypnotherapy technique. I think you'll be surprised and intrigued at what your unconscious mind conjures up.

Think of a small problem you want to change. For example perhaps there is someone you would like to get along with better.

Imagine there are three closed doors in front of you: Door one is labelled, "usual way", door two is labelled, "another person's way" and door three is labelled, "wacky way!"

In a moment you are going to imagine walking through one of those door ways and your unconscious will then present you with a solution or new creative insights.

So as you look at those doors notice which one you are drawn to. Would you prefer to solve the problem in a, "usual way", "another person's way" or a "wacky way!"

And then just allow your unconscious to create an experience behind that door that will give rise to what is known as a "ah ah" eureka moment when you walk through to the other side.

When you feel ready imagine opening the door and walking through, becoming aware of what you are presented with. What do you see, hear, smell and feel? And as you look around what is it that you haven't noticed yet?

You may or may not know at the conscious level how this experience is going to help you, but you can if you wish ask yourself, *"How does this experience help me?"* or *"What new ideas, insights and perspectives does this give me?"*

Whenever we are stuck it's as if our mind is locked into a groove. We can snap out of it and gain creative solutions by accessing the unconscious regions of our mind.

There are many techniques and methods that enable us to achieve this goal such as the 'three magic doors.' Here are some a couple of other ideas for you to practice:

Technique: What's on the back?

1. Picture something you'd like a creative insight into.

2. Have you ever wondered what is on the back of your images?

3. Simply imagine turning the image around and become aware of what is on the back?

Technique: The Wall

1. What is it that you'd like some help with?

2. Imagine a big wall in front of you.

3. Just allow your unconscious or the creative problem solving parts of your mind to manifest some useful insights on the other side of the wall.

4. When you feel ready imagine jumping up and looking over the wall. You may have to jump up a few times to gather all the new information!

Playing around with these kinds of self hypnosis techniques will enable you to learn to access more areas of your mind. And as you continue to do so you will find yourself becoming more capable of solving problems creatively...

How To Solve Relationship Problems With A Jedi Mind Trick

In this short article you too will learn how to solve relationship problems with a 'Jedi Mind Trick.' Relationship problems stem from miscommunication. With the stress and fast pace of modern living this is inevitable. However there are certain time-tested strategies that help you solve relationship problems.

As you read on you will discover the same communication secrets as used by Gandhi in his conflict resolutions, what exceptional therapists and coaches do naturally to gain deep empathy, insight and understanding and what the Buddha taught extensively for developing deep love and compassion.

Wouldn't you agree that in any interaction between two people there are two points of view, right? Well, yes, that's true and there is also a third point of view: Imagining the two of you over there interacting with each other.

These points of view can be called 'Perceptual Positions:'

1st Position (Associated or Self Perspective)

Seeing the situation through your own eyes. You are primarily aware of your own thoughts and feelings.

2nd Position (Other Person Perspective)

Imagining what it is like to be the another person in the interaction. Imagine stepping into their body, seeing through their eyes, hearing through their ears, feeling their feelings and thinking their thoughts.

3rd Position (Disassociated Perspective, Neutral or Meta Position)

Take a detached viewpoint. Imagine you are looking at yourself and the other people in the situation, 'over there'. Try different 'camera angles' to gain new understandings. You could also take the perceptual position of God, Infinite Intelligence etc. for an interesting angle.

You actually shift between these points of view already at an unconscious level, but with conscious intent and practice you can learn how to solve relationship problems more quickly by gaining empathy, insight and rapport with the other person.

Have you ever had the experience of being in an argument with someone and found yourself dumbfounded by the other persons reaction?

Go ahead and think about one of those situations now and run through the following '*Jedi Mind Trick.*' I think you might be surprised by what revelations come up!

Technique: How To Solve Relationship Problems With A Jedi Mind Trick

1. Think of a time when you were in a situation with other people and you didn't and still don't understand their perspectives on whatever issues were discussed. (Examples: A meeting, an argument with someone etc.)

2. Now run through this situation from 1st Position. This means looking at the situation through your own eyes and hearing through your own ears. Notice your feelings and any thoughts you have about it.

3. Next step inside one of the other people present (2nd Position). Literally imagine being in their body looking out of their eyes. So of course you will be able to see yourself. Notice your feelings as you see and hear from this perspective. Become aware of any new learning's!

4. Now move to 3rd position. Remember this is the 'neutral position.' It's kind of as if you are a camera observing everything. See/hear yourself and the others and notice any new learning's you can observe. Try changing 'camera angle.' You can get almost limitless new perspectives. How about, *"Getting above it all?"*, *"A birds eye view?"*

If you've gone through the process you'll have new insights into yourself and you will have a better understanding of others too. Sometimes this technique can be quite a revelation, seeing yourself as others see you enables you to change your behaviour to something more appropriate if necessary.

Keep in mind – If you want another person to change, it's better and easier to change your own behaviour!

NOTE: You can go much further with this process if you meditate down to a deep level of mind – Alpha/Theta Brainwave level. The practice of deep trance identifying with another is one of the teachings that the Buddha taught for cultivating love and compassion for others. I believe he called it, *"exchanging self with others."*

Enriching Your Life Metaphors

The way we walk through the world is heavily influenced by the Neuro-Linguistic models we create in our mind. What this means in plain English is that our experience (which is created by our senses of sight, sound, smell, taste and touch) is transformed into linguistic labels and visual icons/metaphors.

We have to do this generalisation process to be able to cope with the complex nature of reality. Converting our intricate experiences into a visual metaphor enables us to remember that information for quick recollection and processing.

It's true – a picture tells a thousand words.

We create metaphors for all kinds of things. You just have to listen carefully to any conversation and you'll hear them pop out:

- *"I felt like I was on top of the world."*
- *"It felt like a great weight was lifted off my shoulders."*
- *"You are the sunshine of my life."*

You can probably think of your own favourites.

Now where it gets really interesting is with what is known as life metaphors. One of the most well known in recent times was Forrest Gump's, *"Life is like a box of Chocolates…"*

A couple of others:

"My life is like a broken record, things just keep going round and round in a monotonous loop."

"Life is a great big canvas, and you should throw all the paint you can on it." – Danny Kaye

Now because these metaphors represent a generalisation of all aspects of 'life,' when you change this life metaphor, you can change your whole attitude to life!

That's quite powerful right?

So what is your life metaphor? Maybe you have an idea already? You can find out easily enough by asking yourself the following question, "*As I think about it now my life is like...*"

When you describe it, notice the corresponding visual imagery; Where are the images located in space? Is it in colour or black and white? Can you see yourself in it or are you seeing it through your own eyes? Is it still or moving?

Now think about what you would really like your life to be like?

"*Ideally, life to me would be like...*" and notice the visual imagery.

What you can do now is enrich your current life metaphor in a way that heads towards your ideal future.

Picture your current life metaphor and notice the ideal life metaphor at the same time. Now what's the first thing you need to do in that first image to enhance it towards the ideal. What do you need to remove, add or transform?

For example if your current life metaphor is a bit dim and dingy, what happens when you add in some bright spot lights and pan the focus back so you can see, "*the big picture.*"

By playing around with the imagery you can imagine yourself in a little story or journey that goes towards the ideal life. Actually imagine what steps you would need to make to go from A to B. Allow yourself to go through the journey, noticing new insights and other learnings as you change the metaphorical landscape.

This can cause a very beneficial change because you are working directly on your, primarily unconscious, deep structure map of reality! By the way you can solve problems quickly with the use of metaphors as this tool demonstrates.

Technique: What is that like? Metaphors

1. What is your problem like? eg) It's like a brick wall or It's like I'm stuck in mud.

2. Allow yourself to become aware of this internal metaphor. There is a lot of unconscious information in this image that can help you solve the problem. Notice the colours, size, distance, texture. Any sounds?

3. Now what could you do to enhance this imagery? Can you pan back and 'see the bigger picture' ? Or simply add in some blue sky with fluffy clouds and shining sun beams. What happens if you add a soundtrack?

4. Play with this metaphor until you feel something shifting. Often the whole metaphorical image will change at some point.

5. Think about something totally different. And then think of the original problem and notice how it has changed.

Banishing Boredom & Frustration

Here's a simple way to shift your state of mind from boredom and frustration to love, appreciation and gratitude.

Technique: Banish Boredom

1. Place your hands on your heart centre.
2. Close your eyes and gently breath there for a few moments.
3. Now allow yourself to think of five things you are grateful for.
4. Feel that energy of gratitude resonating at your heart centre.

NOTE: If you have more time you could practice what the Buddhists call 'the web of kindness.' This is a worthwhile experience. Start by thinking about one thing you are grateful for. Let's say it's your car. You would now follow the 'web of kindness.' Who sold you the car and handed over the keys and documents? Think about the people that took care of making the safety features work. Think about the people that delivered all the parts. Who built those transporters? Who made the fry ups that they ate along the route? You get the idea. It's infinite of course – The Web of Kindness!

How to Solve Problems and Access Creative Genius with The Wheel of Knowledge (Self Hypnosis Method)

"All Resources are Within"

This has become quite a well known idea but how can you actually make real use of it? We all possess a wealth of unconscious data: Failures we've learned from, success's, dreams, ideas, concepts, beliefs, habits, memories. All of it is available to us if we learn how to access it in the right way. And is it just possible to be able to access information beyond our own unconscious mind?

One of the quickest routes into the unconscious database is with the use of 'empowering questions.' The mind moves in a direction. That is, it is goal orientated. By asking a well formed question you can direct the mind to open up the Gold Mine of Information!

- How can I solve this problem?
- What new creative ideas can I come up with?
- How could I view this in a new empowering way?
- What do I need to do to change this situation around?

Now asking these empowering questions and allowing the answers to start entering into your conscious mind will give you access to new resources. That is great, but how cool would it be if you could go a step further and gain access to the wisdom of genius's?

In Napoleon Hill's classic, "Think & Grow Rich," he talks about using the power of imagination to create a 'Master Mind' group. A person visualises being in a meeting with their chosen role models and imagines communicating with them about their projects, gleaning gold nuggets of insight.

You could of course choose Genius's dead or alive, real or fiction. Doing the imagination experiment and asking good questions some how enables you to unlock amazing creative resources!

Now imagine what would happen if you could get all your favourite genius's and role models together to form a 'Personal Hypnotic Coaching Team.' That would be pretty groovy right?

Have you ever experienced a hypnotic 'double induction'? This is where you have two people on either side of you giving you positive suggestions as you sink into trance. It's quite a profound experience. Don Quan and his Shamanic merry men used to play around with it back in the day…

Anyway I came up with a very neat Self Hypnosis Technique that I call, "The Wheel of Knowledge" that makes use of 'Good Questions,' 'The Master Mind,' 'Hypnotic Double Induction,' and 'Hypnotic Suggestion.'

It's a great technique that enables you to access your inner resources and just possibly from out there! The first thing to do is set your intention. What is the outcome you want to achieve? Then come up with a good question to ask the Genius Role Models.

Technique: The Wheel of Knowledge (Self Hypnosis Method)

1. Relax into Trance

2. Set Intention and think of a good question to ask your Role Models: eg) *"I want to…"*, *"How can I…"*

3. Choose Role Models / Genius's

4. Visualise a Big Wheel (Like the London Eye?) on your Left **and** Right.

5. Place Role Models alternatively left and right onto the Wheels. As you do so establish contact with each Role Model with eye contact. Say Hello.

6. Start hearing answers and suggestions to your Question /Intent.

7. Start moving the wheels while continuing to hear suggestions.

8. As the wheels begins to go faster and faster you won't be able to decipher the 'Double Induction' so just allow your unconscious to integrate the suggestions…

*You may well become confused as the wheel and suggestions spin really fast. That is fine though as confusion often precedes new understanding.

Because this is basically a Self Hypnosis Technique you can expect some interesting things to happen in your future! Look out for spontaneous combustions. Err nope sorry, I mean spontaneous changes and 'ahhh haaa' moments. Pleasant surprises and insights.

And depending on what you intended and asked for, you could have wonderful things happening in your future. Things get unconsciously 'future paced' by the Hypnotic Genius's! So why not give this a go on the Wheel of Knowledge: *"How can I enjoy life even more?"*

How Can I Stop Procrastinating?

We're bombarded with information. We suffer from 'Information Overload.' It's easy to keep putting things off, so you may well ask, *"How Can I Stop Procrastinating?"*

Here's a fact: when you get clear on what you need to get done and prioritise those tasks, your productivity will increase dramatically.

I learned the following strategy from the world-renowned Brain Tracy. It works! Give it a go now:

Technique: Eat That Frog

1. Make a rough list of all the tasks you need to do today.

2. Get a new sheet of paper and at the top write out the number one priority task that you need to get done today. (This is your 'frog.')

3. Now write A, B, C, D underneath and write out your other important tasks by priority.

4. As you do each tasks cross them out or tick them.

*Top Tip: At the end of the day before you go to bed, review what you need to do tomorrow. Write out a new 'Eat That Frog' list. Go to sleep. Review the list first thing in the morning.

So there you go, I hope that's helped you stop procrastinating.

Creative Problem Solving With Visual Metaphors

Do you ever get stuck in a rut? Do you sometimes wish you could snap out of your well worn mental grooves and discover fresh, new and shiny creative Mind Bombs!

When you're stuck in a creative mental block or 'problem state' you are only using a limited portion of your mind. And the fact is the problem remains so because you try to use the same neural circuits to gain creative insight, which is futile. As Einstein famously said:

"The significant problems we have cannot be solved at the same level of thinking with which we created them."

So how can we think about problems or projects from different perspectives in a way that gives rise to useful new understandings?

One of the first things to do is to stop dwelling on the problem. And one of the best ways to do this is to become aware of the structure of the problem. In other words, how does your mind create the problem state: Where are the pictures located in space? How big are they? Are they in colour or black & white?

Focusing on the attributes of your internal thought process's enables you to go to another level of thinking.

Doing this alone can bring about creative insight but you can go much further by manipulating the internal images.

A powerful way to do this is with the use of Metaphorical Images or Icons.

Let's say you were stuck with new ways to move forward with a project. If you were to become aware of your internal images you may see yourself in a small, dim and distant picture looking frustrated…

So if you were to ask yourself, "What is that like?", you may think it is like being stuck in a muddy bog. That becomes your metaphorical image or icon for the 'stuck state.'

What you can then do is remove or add things directly into that image. Play with it and change it. This can be a really nice and easy way of changing unconscious structures which can free up your creative resources.

Below is an excellent technique that enables you to quickly shift problem states into new creative insight utilising the power of metaphorical imagery.

Give it a go now because I think you'll enjoy it!

Technique: Merging Metaphors

(This is a really interesting technique that makes full use of your unconscious resources. You can use it to help you resolve 'stuck states.' Adapted from a technique called 'Spinning Icons' developed by Joe Munshaw and Nelson Zink.)

1. Select a problem state.

2. As you think about your problem state what visual image comes to mind? Notice where it is located in space.

3. Break your current state: eg) Remember you phone number backwards or look up and notice the patterns on the ceiling. Now think about the desired resource state (or outcome, or goal) you would like instead. Notice how you represent this as a visual image. Pay attention to where it is located in space.

4. Now allow your mind to turn the first picture (problem state) into a metaphorical symbol or icon. Keep it in the same location in space. *(This visual metaphor could be quite complex or it may be as simple as a colour. Just trust your unconscious.)*

TOP TIP: It can be useful to ask yourself, *"What is this problem* *state like?*" This often allows a metaphorical representation to arise.

5. Do the same thing with the desired resource state you selected in step 3, making sure to place the new metaphor symbol in the same location in space as the original image.

6. Now see the two metaphor symbols at the same time noticing their locations in space. Next slowly rotate them around each other. Keep rotating them around each other and do so faster and faster. Do this spinning for about 10 seconds allowing the rotation to be so fast that you can no longer track the images and you may even feel a little confused.

7. Now allow the images to merge together, that's right. And push this merged image out in front of you where you can view it easily. Describe the new image briefly, quickly moving to step 8.

8. Immediately begin telling WHATEVER story comes to mind. Just allow yourself to start telling a story. It doesn't matter what it is. It could be a real memory, a story or just simply made up ramblings. The point being is that this process taps into your vast unconscious resources.

9. Now ask yourself, "*How is this story relevant to my problem/challenge?*" or "*How can this story help resolve my problem?*" (This step can help to give you conscious insight into how the previous steps have made some useful changes.)

Did you like that? It's great isn't it! Making use of your own metaphorical icons to shift your internal states is an excellent way to harness the power of your vast unconscious resources.

So what else could you now use this technique on?

Instant Laughter Therapy Exercises

We all suffer from 'over-seriousness' sometimes. It's not surprising really with all the sources of stress in the modern world. Wouldn't it be great to know about instant laughter therapy exercises that you can learn right now!

As you know laughing is the direct opposite to stress. It turns on the para-sympathetic nervous system, releasing feel good chemicals into your blood stream.

So why not give the following 'Instant Laughter Therapy Exercise' a go:

Technique: Instant Laughter Therapy

1. Stand in front of a mirror.

2. Look into your eyes.

3. Start grinning. A big grin. A silly grin. As big as you can!

4. Keep doing this as you allow yourself to start laughing.

Yes it is silly. Doesn't that feel great!

Reduce Stress While Increasing Your Thinking Power Within 5 Minutes

The Fight/Flight/Freeze mechanism is controlled by how much danger we perceive, either real or imagined. Blood begins to leave our 'thinking centre' in the brain and flows into the muscles.

Of course this reduces our thinking power considerably.

Stress causes the neural circuits to get stuck in one region of the brain – the left. The ideal state of mind is to have both hemispheres functioning simultaneously. When you do exercises to stimulate the right-brain it helps to reduce stress and stimulate creative thinking.

Our train of thought is controlled by the questions we ask ourselves. We do this throughout the day, usually at an unconscious level. The amazing thing is your mind, more often than not, answers any question you ask. So better make sure they're good questions right?!

Here's one of the best…

Technique: The Magic Question

"If I did know how to easily solve this problem, how would I?"

By just asking this one question you direct the mind to access it's vast unconscious database of knowledge. Practice asking yourself the magic question and you will quickly create a very useful new habit.

If I were to ask you who your favourite role model is or someone you deeply admire, who would be your first choice? Imagine if you found yourself in their presence being able to ask them anything you wanted!

Well you can; By using the power of your imagination.

It was discovered many years ago that looking up at a 20 degree angle turns your alpha brain wave rhythms on. In this state of mind, your left and right hemispheres are hooked up, giving you access to the whole brain.

In this alpha state it becomes much easier to do creative work like imagining communicating to your favourite 'genius.' With your eyes up at a 20 degree angle, picture your role model in front of you. Say '*Hello!*' and ask, "*How could I understand this better?*" or "*How could I solve problem x ?*"

Thank the person in front of you for their help, just like you would a real person. Shake their hand. This of course can help you gain even more rapport with the genius.

If you enjoy this kind of thought experiment you may want to take it a stage further...

Noticing your role model in front of you, imagine taking their head and placing it onto your own shoulders, rather like you are wearing a helmet. You can then see through their eyes, hear their thoughts and feel their feelings.

In the world of hypnosis this process is known as Deep Trance Identification and can often give you amazing insights and perspectives leading to new solutions.

Here are some useful questions to ask when you have the role models head on:

- *"How can I view this problem in a new empowering way?"*
- *"How can I solve this problem?"*
- *"What else can I learn about this?"*
- *"What's surprising about problem x ?"*

So if you've got a few minutes why not give these ideas a go. You never know you may discover a break-through solution to one of your projects, learning how to de-stress fast at the same time!

Further Life Changing Metaphor Exercises

The way we live our life is often described with the use of metaphors and idioms. When you really pay attention you'll often hear them flying out of peoples mouths:

- *"He's just treading water."*
- *"I felt like I was on top of the world!"*
- *"She's walking on thin ice."*

There are around 25,000 idiomatic expressions in the English language. I'm sure there are many you are familiar with and use yourself everyday. Of course they're often spoken at an unconscious level.

When you take the time to investigate the metaphorical imagery behind the utterance you'll discover it is in fact rich with meaning. This is known as semantic density or put more simply, *"A picture tells a thousand words."*

Usually idiomatic statements are just spoken without paying conscious attention to the actual imagery behind them. However you can become aware of the unconscious right-brain information to your benefit.

You may be aware of some of your metaphors already. Or you can pick one area of your life such as work, relationships, spirituality and so on and then simply ask, *"And what is that like?"*

Give yourself time to answer the question and notice what arises in your mind's eye. For example let's say you picked 'my spiritual life.' When you asked, "What is that like?", you became aware of a winding path going upwards; The spiritual path of course.

If you've ever done any sort of 'Metaphor Work' before you may be tempted to visualise strolling down the path to discover what is at the end, delighting in the rainbows and Unicorns along the way...

However as I learned from Andrew T. Austin's excellent, 'Metaphors of Movement' course recently, it is best to know where you stand first. If you were lost in the wrong side of town in a foreign speaking country, it would be wise to find out exactly where you ARE first.

So staying with the path metaphor, start by looking at your feet in the imagery. And then look forward – What can you see? How far ahead does the scenery go? What is to your left? How far can you see? And the right? And then what is behind you?

Exploring the metaphor this way enables you to get a clear picture of where you currently stand. You can now test the boundaries of the internal landscape. What happens if you step to the left off the path? What happens if you step to the right side of the path? And what happens if you turn around and face the opposite direction?

Give this a go. Just explore the imagery gently noticing what you can see in each direction. You may be tempted to change the image or add things in like you've learned in other metaphor exercises, but resist this and just notice what is there. Remember it represents information from the previously unconscious levels of your mind. It is the deep structure of your metaphorical statements.

Utilising Transcendental States To Solve Problems

If your interested in new problem solving ideas, I think you'll enjoy the following tool that helps you solve problems by making use of transcendental resource states.

Technique: Transcending Problems

1. Access your Resource State

Remember a Peak Experience you once had. Maybe it was a spiritual experience. What about the first time you fell in love? How about that time you looked up at the heavens on a perfectly clear night!

Access it fully and completely. See what you saw at the time, hear what you heard and feel those amazing feelings!

Now anchor this feeling by repeating the sound, *"Wow, wow, wow!"* to yourself.

2. Your Problem State

Think about a project you've got a creative block on. What's the first thing that happens? Slow down and notice… Do you say something to yourself first or do you make an image first? What's the next part of the recipe?

eg) Self Talk, *"errrr, I just don't know what to do!"* ==> See dim and distant Image of yourself looking lost ==> And then feel confused and lost.

3. Break State

Now think about something totally different. What did you have for breakfast? Or look around and notice any red objects.

4. Re-programming Your Thinking Strategy

Now think about your problem again and as soon as you've started interrupt the pattern by repeating loud and clear in your mind the positive resource anchor, *"Wow, wow, wow!"*

5. Repeat several times from Step-3

Notice how your feelings have changed when you think about the challenge now. What new insights and revelations are on there way?

Further Reading

If you found this book useful you will probably enjoy my Amazon Best Seller, *"Boost Your Mind Power: 99+ Awesome Mind Power Techniques"*:

Amazon.com/dp/B0095SQ714

You can also visit my Amazon Author Page:

Amazon.com/Colin-G-Smith/e/B00A3HEKOM

Made in the USA
Middletown, DE
16 June 2019